ROI on Human Capital Investment

ROI

On Human Capital Investment

Second Edition

by

Michael E. Echols

TAPESTRY PRESS
ARLINGTON, TEXAS

Tapestry Press
2000 E. Lamar
Suite 600
Arlington, TX 76006

Printed in the U.S.A.
09 08 07 06 05   1 2 3 4 5

Library of Congress Cataloging-in-Publication Data
Echols, Michael E., 1942-
  ROI on human capital investment / by Michael E. Echols.-- 2nd ed.
      p. cm.
  Summary: "The author suggests means of applying accounting principles
toward the measurement of return on investment in human capital"--Provided
by publisher.
  Includes bibliographical references and index.
  ISBN 1-930819-45-5 (trade paper : alk. paper)
  1. Human capital--Cost effectiveness. 2. Rate of return. I. Title.
  HD4904.7.E29 2005
  658.15'24--dc22
                                                2005022930

Book design and layout by
D. & F. Scott Publishing, Inc.
N. Richland Hills, Texas

Contents

Introduction

The corporate market of ideas is abuzz with the language of return on investment (ROI) on the money being spent by corporations to educate and develop employees—what I call *human capital investment*. Unfortunately, little progress has been made on how and what to measure so that corporations can make these investments based upon their financial value to the corporation.

This book presents a new and different approach to the problem. It is only fair to the reader to share the context from which these ideas have emerged, namely the background and experience of the author.

I am educated as a scientist, having earned a Bachelor of Science degree in physics from Carnegie Mellon University and a PhD from the University of California at Berkeley. My doctoral research focused on mathematical model building and management sciences under my intellectual mentor, Dr. C. West Churchman. My understanding of the role of the chief executive officer (CEO), and in particular the relationship between the CEO and the chief financial officer (CFO), comes from having been a general manager (profit and loss [P&L] responsibility) in the General Electric Company (GE), the president of a GE subsidiary, and the president of a stand-alone chemical company. Lastly, I have been an educator during two separate stages of my career. It was those experiences that helped me appreciate the true importance of learning.

Today, I am the vice president of strategic initiatives at Bellevue University. The charter of the Strategic Initiatives program at Bellevue University is to work with major corporations to create educational programs that align with the business objectives of each corporate client. As I listen to the executives of these corporations, I hear their needs expressed with phrases like, *growing uncertainty, cultural transformation, creative, flexible organization, innovative and risk taking.* At the end of the day, these executives are looking for ways to manage what they see as their most important asset—their people. The goal of this book is to model the issues of strategic human capital investment in order to provide senior management with the tools needed to more effectively deploy corporate resources.

The book is organized by management topics with cross-referencing to support concepts in the other chapters. I've chosen to use this approach in recognition of scarcity of the readers' time.

For further information, go to:
www.humancapitalinvestment.net

Why Human Capital
Investments Matter

Human capital is critical to company financial performance, and how to invest in it is a major challenge for senior management. This book focuses on this challenge and defines the important data required to improve the ROI on human capital investment decision making. The impact of human capital on business performance has been growing and is predicted to continue to grow. In 1900, only 17 percent of all jobs required knowledge workers. Knowledge workers are employees who are valuable for what they do with their ideas rather than what they do with their bodies. Now, over 60 percent of the jobs demand the skills and competencies of an educated work force.[1] In the face of this basic driver of demand, the outlook for the related supply of labor is poor. The immediate period through the year 2008 is especially critical. The Bureau of Labor Statistics predicts that by 2008, 25 percent of senior management positions will be vacant, mostly due to the retirement of baby boomers.[2]

The supply of candidates to fill the vacancies is equally grim. Although the size of the total work force in the United States will grow a total of 12 percent between 1998 and 2008, the number of twenty-five to forty-five-year-olds, the primary pool for future managerial talent, will decline 6 percent during the same period.[3] Another trend is that talented young managers are 60 percent more likely to leave their employer than older managers.[4] This increased mobility is, at least in part, a result of the severing of the traditional loyalty bonds between the employer and the employee—learned by sons and daughters as they watched their parents get "downsized" after years of faithful service to a single employer. The intersection of demand and supply in human capital markets is not a speculation. The data has been derived from existing public demographic records. An excellent summary of the demographic and recruiting issues is available in the article "The Race for Talent: Retaining and Engaging Workers in the 21st Century."[5]

The macroeconomic factors affecting human capital markets are not the only critical elements to be taken into consideration. The growing impact of human capital is clearly seen in the standard accounting reports—the income statement and the balance sheet. Labor costs are the single largest expense for U.S. businesses.

In addition to income statement impact, the shifts in the balance sheet that are related to human capital are equally compelling. Data show that traditional accounting rules are increasingly inadequate instruments to manage and predict company market value. In 1982, tangible assets (balance sheet assets) represented 62 percent of a U.S. corporation value on average. By 1992, this figure had dropped to 38 percent. More recent studies estimate that the tangible assets of corporations account for as little as 15 percent of average market value of publicly traded American companies.[6] In other words, in some cases only 15 percent of U.S. corporate market value is accounted for by the tangible assets documented on the balance sheet. The balance, or 85 percent of the value, is related to intangible assets (assets that do not appear on the balance sheet), which includes the human capital of the enterprise.

The important result here is that traditional CFO accounting rules are providing less and less guidance for managers involved in investment decision making. With the diminished importance of traditional accounting measurements in the valuation of the company, executive investment decision making needs new measurements to guide those investment decisions. This is most critical when it comes to the company's most important asset—its people.

The financial impact resulting from strategic investment in training and education is equally well documented in several highly reputable research studies. Figure 1.1 lists conclusions from three of these studies.

Figure 1.1

▶ **McKinsey and Company**: Companies that scored in the top 20 percent of our talent management index on average have 22 percentage points higher return to stockholders than their industry peers.

▶ **Accenture**: This study measured the overall business impact of the learning function. High performance companies produce higher operating results:

Sales per employee	27% greater
Revenue growth	40% greater
Income growth	50% greater

▶ **American Society for Training and Development (ASTD)**: Average five-year returns in stock market value related to level of company training investment:

Top 50 firms produced	86% return
Standard & Poors (S&P) firms produced	25% return
Bottom 50 firms produced	19% return

Yet even with these documented relationships between human capital investment and superior financial performance, investment in human capital is actually declining in a number of important areas. The obvious question is, "what is going on here?" The arguments for strategically managing investments in human capital are compelling at the macroeconomic level, the microeconomic level, and the performance level; yet, "most companies and leaders appear reluctant to invest in talent. Companies often spend millions on moderately high-risk capital projects with four to five-year paybacks yet balk at spending a fraction of that on more and better people."[7] It is the core thesis of this book that accounting methods used for capital investment in tangible asset allocation decisions provide a valuable analytical foundation, but that those methods are incomplete for human capital investment decision making. To the distress of senior managers and investors alike, existing measurements in their current form do not translate into useful tools for intangible asset investment decision making, especially those involving human capital and talent.

Rigorous analytical tools for human capital investment decisions are required. The identification of critical parameters is needed to guide decision making. Once those parameters have been defined, the challenge to the company is to develop management processes to measure and track the value of these parameters for their business. These parameters and their use in the associated decision models become the basis for holding individual managers accountable for outcomes and performance related to human capital investment decisions.

The first evidence to be examined is the data on the expenditures (i.e., the investment (I) portion of the ROI calculation). Expenditures for training declined 6 percent in 2003.[8] *Training* magazine reports a slight decline in the corporate training market.[9] Data from the ASTD 2003 and 2004 State of the Industry reports decline in training expenditures of Benchmark Forum companies ASTD surveys annually. The ASTD Benchmark Forum group consists of some Fortune 500 companies and large public-sector organizations that share detailed data on their spending and practices each year. Training expenditures for Benchmark Forum companies as a percentage of payrolls were down from 2.47 percent in 2002 to 1.99 percent in 2004.[10] Because the percentage is calculated on total payroll, these declines represent a large decrease in absolute dollars expended by Benchmark Forum companies.

One of the first questions to be considered is, "how much are companies really investing in human capital?" The answer is a lot; but after that the precision decreases drastically. Some academic researchers report that American corporations are spending a total of between $16 billion and $55 billion annually for employee development.[11] Few corporate expenditure categories have an estimated range that varies by this magnitude.

One immediate implication of this variance is that quantitative measures of human capital ROI have a long way to go. The investment (I) portion of the ROI calculation should be the easiest variable to measure. A range of more than 300 percent can hardly be classified as precise. To start, we must have a more precise measure of this critical variable.

This lack of precision extends to the more than $10 billion spent annually for tuition reimbursement. When asked about the management of tuition reimbursement resources, Dr. John Sullivan, professor of management at San Francisco State University and an expert in measurements related to human resources, is more than a little passionate. In *Workforce Management*, May 2004,[12] Dr Sullivan says, "What's odd is that companies don't know what they're spending (on tuition reimbursement) and furthermore, don't seem to care. It's the dumbest thing I've ever heard of." Companies not only don't know the return on human capital investments, many don't know the investment. In the case of tuition reimbursement expenditures, many companies do not have precise measurements of the investment portion of the calculation.

As a result, the lack of precision about expenditure levels is one of the factors that adversely affect executive confidence in human capital investment decisions. It is reflected in management comments. Only 16 percent of surveyed senior executives are satisfied with the overall performance of their training organization.[13]

As large as the investment is, chapter 9 below provides analysis that indicates that companies may actually be under investing in human capital. Uncertainty is one of the culprits. Investment literature documents the impact of uncertainty on investment behavior. The greater the uncertainty, the greater the reluctance to tie up resources in long-term investments. With the decline in training expenditures, which were noted earlier, combined with the increase in the importance of difficult to measure intangible assets, it is likely that growing uncertainty is indeed a culprit in reduced investment activity.

One thing is clear. The problem is not the availability of funds. As the importance of intangible assets grows, American corporations continue to accumulate cash—the balance sheet item that generates the lowest ROI of all the capital assets (average annual return over five years on U. S. money market instruments was 2 percent[14]). "Instead of investing, corporate America has been accumulating cash—big piles of it. According to the most recent figures from the Federal Reserve Board, non-financial corporations increased their liquid assets by 20 percent, to a record $1.3 trillion (10 percent of the total economy), from the start of 2003 to June 2004."[15] The title of the article, "Long on Cash, Short on Ideas," is at the heart of the issue.

Dr. Edward Lawler, in his work *Creating a Strategic Human Resources Organization,* says, "Effective talent strategy may be the most important HR contribution to business strategy."[16] The point is reinforced in additional literature: "The owners of intangible capital have the potential to capture much of the returns while making much less of a financial investment—and without taking much of the risk."[17] Unfortunately McKinsey and Co. documents the current state of affairs in *The War for Talent*, a publication based upon answers to 6,000 completed questionnaires from senior managers in seventy-seven large American companies. Only 20 percent of the surveyed executives agreed that they have enough talented leaders to pursue most of their companies' business opportunities.[18]

Why We Need to Change the Way We're Doing Business

The organizational focal point for the issue of investment in human capital is the human resources (HR) department. In the war over corporate resources, HR is clearly losing the battle. Today, HR departments are often viewed as not being strategic in a fast-moving global economy where increased competition applies pressure for ever more precise data to make resource allocation decisions. Without measurable data to back its arguments for corporate investment resources, the HR department is missing the credibility to advance innovative recommendations, especially when those recommendations are critiqued relative to the highly precise decision rules of accounting. The profession has been amply self-critical, while senior executive opinion could at best be characterized as mixed. HR needs to get onto the playing field with the CFO. The only alternative is to engage senior management on the field of ROI using objective data.

In a survey of HR and operating managers that appeared in the publication *Human Resources Executive* (October 2, 2003), the gap between importance of an activity and performance of that activity was measured. The gap is defined as the percentage of those people surveyed who think an activity is important, minus the percent of those surveyed who feel current performance is acceptable. On the dimension of executive and management development, the HR manager's gap was negative 48 percentage points, while the operating manager's gap was negative 51 percentage points.[19] The good news is that operating managers and HR professionals agree. The bad news is that the gap between importance and performance is unfavorable and huge. Much of the debate on how to rectify the situation revolves around ROI—a measurement some consider unattainable in the management of human capital investments.

Measurement of ROI has the potential to change the way corporations allocate resources needed to develop their people. The change required is to stop accounting for human capital expenditures as overhead expenses in the category of health-care expenses, vacation time, and holidays. When P&L pressures are being felt, these overhead expenditures are the first to be cut. Training expenditures are no exception. Accounting for human capital investments must become more like capital investment accounting, where the return on current period expenditures is relative to the return earned over the useful life of the asset. Treating money spent to develop human capital as a current period expense results in tremendous variability in practices, policies and procedures. The constant pressure is to reduce costs and best *investment* practices are conspicuously absent.

The traditional corporate policy used to manage tuition reimbursement as a benefit and book it as a current period expense is examined in detail. Tremendous variability exists even with this policy. Only 16 percent of companies impose a financial obligation on the employee to pay back some or all of the tuition reimbursement benefit in the event the employee leaves the firm within a specified time period of receiving the benefit—a term called handcuffs in the cited reference.[20] The financial implications of such policies are examined in later chapters dealing with the financial model. The current use of this policy is not even directly related to the size of the benefit. The company studied in the cited Benson et al research revised its tuition reimbursement policy in 1996. The company has no handcuffs as part of its tuition reimbursement policy. Under the new policy, the company pays 100 percent of all employee tuition costs independent of subject studied, cost per credit or length of employment obligation. In addition, employees are given a few hours per week off the job for study. Finally, the company mentioned in the study awards $10,000 worth of company common stock upon award of a degree irrespective of level or domain of the degree awarded.[21]

The company studied by Benson et al invests heavily in its human capital and is a rare exception among American corporations. Some companies split the costs with the employee. Both The Schwan Food Company and The Battelle Institute proportion the tuition costs at an 80:20 ratio with the company paying the 80 percent share. Other companies manage the benefit through annual caps. At General Motors, the yearly limit is $6,400 per individual for undergraduate education and $10,000 for postgraduate courses; Washington Trust caps its assistance at $5,000 per year per employee.[22]

The annual cap approach has some immediate implications. If the employee enrolls in degree courses that cost a total $7,000 in a given benefit year and the corporate annual tuition reimbursement cap is $5,250, that is all that will be paid against the education costs. First Data Corporation (FDC) uses this approach. Under this common scenario, the student has no opportunity to carry over the balance of the investment of $1,750 ($7,000 –$5,250) into the next fiscal year. Under most policies, the employee is not qualified to be reimbursed against next year's annual benefit cap of $5,250.

The use of an annual cap is important to help the corporation both cap and manage the level of expenditures in a given year. However, such policies have an unintended side

effect. These policies prohibit an *investment* strategy comparable to tangible asset investments where large investments
are capitalized over multiple years in the future. The point is
that the total level of human capital investments made in any
year should be defined by the need for the asset as dictated by
future competitive forces, not by an arbitrary policy created
to minimize benefit expenses in a given year. The semblance
of a multiyear policy is the one used by Caterpillar, Inc (CAT).
CAT has a total lifetime employment tuition benefit of
$25,000. This policy allows the payment of the imputed sec-
ond-year balance of $1,750 in the $7,000 total example, thus
creating a crude simulation of the multiyear characteristic of
balance sheet asset investments.

What is most striking about these different approaches to tuition reimbursement policy is the variability between companies. Intuitively, it must be the case
that some approaches are better than others. However,
there is no well-defined criterion for measurement that
would allow conclusions about what policy is better or
worse than another policy relative to a set of business
objectives. This issue will be addressed in greater detail in
chapter 7, where various policy options are evaluated
using the ROI measurements developed here.

Accounting literature presents the first challenge to
calculating ROI on human capital investment. The issue is
the very definition of an asset. *The Managerial Auditing
Journal* poses the question, "should investments in people
be treated as assets?" The main criteria for the accountants to classify an asset include the following:

- ▶ It must possess future service potential.
- ▶ It must be measurable in monetary terms.
- ▶ It must be subject to the ownership or control of
  the accounting entity.[23]

The first two criteria present practical economic challenges to the measurement of the ROI on human capital
investments. These two criteria are dealt with in detail in

the financial model presented in later chapters. The implications of the third criterion are that humans cannot be viewed as assets unless they are owned. Unlike the two economic criteria, this is a philosophical and moral question, one at the heart of some of the most troubling issues ever faced by our nation.

The issue of human ownership was ducked by the founding fathers in the drafting of the U.S. Constitution, only to be ultimately resolved between 1861 and 1865 at a cost of 600,000 lives—the price paid by our ancestors during the American Civil War. Surely modern day accountants do not advocate the reversal of this earlier expenditure of the nation's blood as the price to be paid in order to address the management of important strategic human capital assets in the modern era. More enlightened definitions are required before investments in human capital can be given serious consideration by the CEO and the CFO.

> Definition of investment: The process of exchanging income during one period of time for an asset that is expected to produce earnings in future periods.[24]

> Definition of asset: 1. Valuable thing—a property to which value can be assigned. 2. Somebody or something that is useful and contributes to the success of something.[25]

Both of these definitions are sufficiently comprehensive to provide utility when applied to human capital. It can only be hoped that these broader definitions are acceptable to senior executives as operational foundations for removing the current roadblocks to ROI measurement.

The first challenge is to develop more consistent approaches to managing resource allocation. Examination of financial measurements, which link the CFO to the CEO in resource allocations, is a valuable place to refine the definitions needed in the investment in human capital. One quantification that links the current funds flow to a plan for the future is a budget. Budgets are most familiar as planning instruments applied to investments in tangible assets. The fixed asset budgets have some highly recognizable characteristics that relate directly to a plan of action. Examination of a few of these investment characteristics serves as a useful platform for the investment side of the human capital question.

Table 2.1
Characteristics of Tangible Asset Investments

► Annual investment growth in plant and equipment is roughly proportional to the growth in volume and sales of the company. When the potential exists to sell more cars, additional capacity is budgeted by the automaker to build a new plant and purchase the new equipment needed to produce those cars. The auto manufacturer creates a plan along with a multiyear budget precisely because the investment that is required to create the asset spans more than a single year.

Note: Development of human capital is, in fact, a multiyear proposition even though it is most often accounted for as a single period cost.

► Discontinuities in the competitive landscape, changes in the characteristics of served markets, new market potential or rapid changes in the technology come from outside the company and require changes in resource allocations. The company's response can be critical to survival. Such external impacts require either a significant increase in the investment budget or a radical shift in budgeted resource allocation to respond to the specific external threats.

► Forecasted business outcomes, such as productivity improvements, expanded output, yield improvements, et cetera, and the measurement of financial outcomes relative to a budget are a part of investment justification to the CFO. Evaluations of the outcomes relative to forecasted values are done after the investment has been completed and the results have been measured.

These results are actually the return (R) portion of the ROI while the budget is the planned level of the investment (I) portion of the allocation decision.

► The level of management review of a tangible asset investment proposal is directly related to the size of the investment proposal and/or the criticality of the investment to the financial performance of the business. Low-level investment authorization is delegated to middle managers who have responsibility for production. Investments that require large amounts of capital or have critical strategic significance often make it all the way to the board of directors.

Note: Authorization for the individual expenditure of the tuition reimbursement benefits are usually delegated to the lowest level of management immediately above the employee. Higher levels of management get involved only when the aggregate total of the delegated expenditures reach a cumulative level that exceeds a cap set to control expenses.

► Virtually all operating manager requests for tangible asset expansion require an ROI analysis that links the expected future returns to current period expenditure. ROI values above a corporate screening threshold define the attractiveness of the investment under management consideration. The future expected benefits are virtually always expressed in dollars.

Note: Calculation of the return (R) on human capital investment based on dollars is one of the huge challenges for managers from the top to the bottom of corporations.

► The cash expenditure for tangible assets, such as buildings and equipment are most often capitalized by multiyear financing agreements such as bonds or loans that define retirement of the associated debt through staged payments executed over future years.

Note: Tuition reimbursement is virtually always booked as a current year expense.

The detailed examination of the management of tuition reimbursement benefits further focuses the discussion. In table 2.2, current approaches used widely to manage this benefit are titled "benign neglect." Dimensions of this approach are compared with those required for investment decision making.

Table 2.2
Tuition Reimbursement Policy
Investment vs. Benign Neglect

Business Issue	Investment	Benign Neglect
Year over year growth in total	Proportional to sales	Flat, down, or random
Shifts in skill needs driven by competition, technology, or market changes	Plan to accelerate skills developed jointly between operations and HR	No discussions or plans
Financial results	Measurements	No data
Level of review	CEO/Board review of large budget/plans	Neither pre nor post review outside of HR

In addition to the financial dimensions, behavior is critical in human capital. From the McKinsey and Co. work *The War for Talent*: "Managers told us they want the company to help them develop their skills. This is particularly important today, as people realize that the only career security lies in the collection of skills and experience that they bring to the job market."[26] The demise of job security created a new career model—Me, Inc.—which eliminated loyalty to employers.[27] The research has even more definitive data on the issue of personal development as it relates to behavior in the workplace.

▶ Managers who feel their company develops them poorly are five times more likely to leave than people who feel their company develops them well.
▶ Fifty-seven percent of managers who intend to leave their current employer in the next two years cited insufficient development and learning opportunities as a major reason for leaving.[28]
▶ In surveys of adult learners, 85 percent named career transitions as their reasons for deciding to learn.[29] Of those, the large majority of adult students (about 70 percent) enroll in degree programs. They most often seek a bachelor's degree (44 percent), followed by a master's degree (27 percent) and an associate's degree (25 percent).[30]

As a result of this data, the next chapters focus on the investment of tuition reimbursement resources as they are applied to degree programs related to career advancement.

3 Human Capital—A Twenty-First-Century Oxymoron

The success factors in human capital investment are distinct from success factors in tangible asset capital investments. Here we introduce concepts and language to enhance the tools to manage *human* capital investment.

The phrase *human capital* is embedded in the business literature. A few examples make the point.

"Discounting traditional analysis of earnings derived from physical capital and replacing it with analysis of earnings power derived from *human capital*."[31]

"An increasingly competitive global economy and the realization that *human capital* is the key to organizational performance . . ."[32]

"What matters in the new economy, however, is *human capital*."[33]

Taking a step back to examine the commonly used phrase human capital is vital to the rigorous analysis of ROI on human capital investment. The battle is engaged when the HR manager represents the human agenda of the company's relationship with the employees while at the same time the CFO represents the hard-nosed financial reality of the competitive markets. Both make resource allocation recommendations to their CEO.

The only hope for the HR manager is to move toward the strong position held by the CFO where numbers win out over mushy words. Namely, human capital investment

decisions need to look more like capital investment decisions—they need to have an ROI to compete with all of the
other requests for corporate resources.

The CFO measurements are defined by the rules of
accounting. One of the foundations of accounting is the
principle of objectivity. Physical assets are accounted for at
historical costs rather than current market value precisely
because historical costs are measured objectively on the
basis of a third-party market transaction. This accounting
decision rule removes all subjectivity from the measurement. The very definition of objective warms the cockles of
the accountant's heart.

> Definition of *objective*: Free of any bias or prejudice
> caused by personal feelings. Based on facts rather than
> thoughts or opinions.[34]

Additional clarity is available from the *Merriam-Webster
Online Dictionary*.

> Definition of *objective*: Relating to, or being an object,
> phenomenon, or condition in the realm of sensible
> experience independent of individual thought and per-
> ceptible by *all* observers: having reality independent of
> the mind . . .[35]

The essence of the accounting priority is founded on the
Merriam-Webster phrase *dealing with facts or conditions as
perceived without distortion by personal feelings, prejudices, or interpretations*. The practical implications follow
from the objective principles of accounting in the root
phrase *capital investment*.

> Definition of *capital investment*: Money that is spent on
> buildings and equipment to increase the effectiveness
> of a business.[36]

This definition only accommodates objects such as buildings and equipment. Here there is no room for the human
being at all since the essence of humanity is subjective. In
addition, humans are endowed with free will, adding a

further uncertainty to the financial calculations. Because free will creates risk for the corporation, it is an important concept to be examined in detail in later chapters.

We now turn our attention to the second initiating decision maker in the drama of human capital investment decisions, namely the HR manager. The conflict with the CFO begins with the very title of this new player that has so recently walked upon the stage of corporate resource allocation decisions. The human assets can no longer be ignored because the importance of the physical assets the CFO can measure has declined in relative importance from 62 percent to about 15 percent of the total value of the corporation (see chapter 1 for specifics).

The conflict begins with the very title of the HR manager, namely *human*.

The essence of human is about the personal—about the feelings, prejudices, and interpretations of the individual. The essence of structural conflict is captured in the word *subjective*.

> Definition of *subjective*: Relating to or being experience or knowledge as conditioned by personal mental characteristics or states.[37]

It is not possible to even conceive of a more dramatic juxtaposition to the essence of accounting. The conflicting positions of the two executives are worthy of the very definition of tragedy in a Shakespearean play. In the absence of some new approach, the relationship between the two is doomed from the outset. No wonder the CEO is frustrated as he (she) tries to reconcile the conflicting advice of these two managers. It is as though the CFO and the HR manager are speaking two different languages. The bottom line is that the very phrase *human capital* may be the ultimate executive suite oxymoron.

At the moment, the language of the CFO holds the upper hand in resource allocation discussions based upon familiarity and historical precedent. The challenge is to define the critical new concepts and the associated language that inserts the human into the capital investment decisions while preserving the maximum degree of objectivity required to make the ROI calculation credible for the CEO and the rightfully skeptical CFO.

Key Concepts and Associated Language
1. Coinvestor
In the case of tangible asset investments, the corporation is the *sole investor*. In the human capital investment of the tuition reimbursement resources, the human is actually a *coinvestor* with the corporation. As in any joint venture, the individual interests of the investors have some shared elements as well as some conflicting interests.

The coinvestor status is true even in those cases where the corporate tuition reimbursement benefit is 100 percent of all financial outlays. Without the concurrent employee investment of the human elements of their time, motivation, and emotional energy, the dollar investment is a wasted expenditure with very low potential of producing economic benefit to the company. Development of strategy and policies to secure coinvestor status in human capital investments is a necessary prerequisite to producing an ROI for the corporation.

The HR policies of the corporation further preclude the company from being the sole investor of the more than $10 billion of capital available in tuition reimbursement resources. Even though the HR department is managing the disbursements of these resources, they are under the control of the employee. Only the employee can initiate the expenditure. In the absence of a conscious decision on the part of the employee to actually use the benefit, the corporation has no power to make the investment in the first place. Thus, in sharp contrast with tangible asset investments, the employee ultimately controls the human capital investment decision when it comes to the $10 billion of investment in tuition reimbursement. This reality is especially annoying to the CFO, who historically has been the ultimate decision maker in all tangible asset capital investments.

2. Free Will

Chapter 1 introduced the concept of ownership in the accountant definition of asset. In the case of human assets, as in, "people are our most important asset," America has institutionalized the concept of free will in the seminal documents of the Declaration of Independence and the Constitution.

The practical implication of this cultural and political constraint on human capital investments must be dealt with in a structural way that accommodates the objectivity criterion of the CFO to the maximum degree feasible. In chapter 6, which deals with ROI to the corporation, the financial implications of free will are modeled.

3. Multiple Return Periods

In chapter 2, we introduced the requirement that both investment and asset require multiperiod analysis. Under current HR and CFO policies, tuition reimbursement costs are booked as current period expenses. To qualify for multiperiod analysis, the corporate ROI calculation on human capital investment must account for return [R] in future periods discounted by the appropriate interest rate. The return in the future period t is defined as R_t and the current discounted value of the period t return is R_t divided by the period discount factor. The term is:

$$R_t/(1 + \text{interest rate})^t \qquad t = 1, 2, 3 \ldots$$

4. Objective Return Measurement

Some past studies on ROI in training programs fall short of credibility because the return measurement R is based on subjective inputs. This represents a migration from objective to subjective that is unacceptable for the CFO. In her analysis of return on investment in training, "Measuring the Employer's Return on Investment in Training: Evidence from the Literature," Ann Bartel documents ROI values that range from zero to 5,900 percent.[38] The only way such variability in values can occur is as a result of the methodology used to define outcomes—the "R" in the ROI calculation.

The primary sources for the "R" terms in this book are the market-defined average salaries paid for employees with a high school degree, some post secondary credits, a bachelor's degree or a master's degree.

Thus, it is in the intersection between the subjective and the objective where the challenge to provide the CFO and the CEO with acceptable ROI on human capital investment measurement is played out. Here the minimally sufficient parameters required to bridge the gap are defined and defended for usage in the chapters to follow.

4

The No-Brainer Investment
for the Employee

A nalysis reveals that the return on investment to the employee is both large and attractive. Although the quantitative value of the ROI calculation gives clear definition to the financial implications of the calculation, the form of the analysis provides an important foundation for analyzing corporate policy alternatives. Each case discussed examines the impact of various decisions made by the individual and the corporation. It also creates the basis for the corporate ROI calculation presented in chapter 6.

Two financial dimensions are derived in this first set of calculations. These are the dimensions:

1. Asset value
2. Income stream

Table 4.1
Market Return Data

U.S. Census Bureau: "Educational Attainment in the United States: 2003"[39]

Average Annual Income, 2002

High school degree holder	$27,280
Bachelor's degree holder	$51,194
Advanced degree	$71,820

Education is an asset that simply keeps on producing value for the individual. Once a person has earned a degree, his or her earning potential is permanently improved. Thus, an ROI-based investment model requires a multi-period return horizon. This represents a departure from the single period expensing model currently used by the vast majority of organizations to account for tuition reimbursement. The ROI in the increased value of the employee's personal asset is more than 400 percent with details on the calculations and assumptions in appendix A.

With the ROI to the employee over 400 percent when all of the tuition costs are paid directly by the employee, it is a logical conclusion that the return on the employee's out-of-pocket expenses can only increase with tuition reimbursement benefits supplied by the corporation. The corporate tuition reimbursement benefits reduce the denominator of the ROI calculation while the numerator stays the same. Table 4.2 shows these results.

Table 4.2
Employee ROI Under Tuition Reimbursement Plan

Corporation pays zero tuition reimbursement:	Employee ROI = 400%+
Corporation pays 80% of tuition:	Employee ROI = 2,500%+

The ROI calculations show that the securing of a bachelor's degree is a very attractive investment for the employee under every financial scenario. The various corporate reimbursement policies merely move the returns from incredible to ridiculously incredible. The conclusion that investment in a bachelor's degree is one of the most attractive investment opportunities the employee will have in his or her lifetime holds, no matter what portion of the cost is paid by the corporation.

Although the return on investment is unambiguous, there is often a lack of correlation between the financial results and employee behavior. Even for the company in the Benson et al study, where the employee ROI is infinite and $10,000 in stock awaits employees who get a degree, less than 50 percent of the employees took advantage of the tuition reimbursement benefit during the 4.5-year study period.[40] Not every employee takes advantage of the only "no-brainer" investment opportunity he will ever have, no matter how attractive the corporate offer to fund the investment.

Based on these results, it is highly likely that the corporation's tuition reimbursement policy acts as a facilitator to the employee education decision but doesn't serve as the primary motivator. Corporate tuition assistance policies do not alter the asset value of having the degree. The value is defined in the open market, not by the corporate tuition reimbursement policy. Thus, although corporate tuition reimbursement policy might increase the percentage of employees enrolling in degree-seeking activity, it does not alter the market value of the knowledge obtained.

Given these compelling financial results, the obvious question is, why doesn't every employee make the investment to get his degree? In the absence of more complete data, the best we can do is define some of the important barriers to employee coinvestment in education.

Barrier 1: Incomplete Market Information
The employee simply does not know the market value of a degree, as reflected in table 4.1.

Barrier 2: Employee Does Not Expect to Realize Actual Cash Flow From the Asset Value
The employee ROI measures the external market value of the asset. In the absence of a willingness to assertively negotiate for that value, transformation from asset value

to cash is difficult. There are no assurances that the employee will receive salary increases from the current employer commensurate with the increased asset value. If the employee expects to remain with his current employer, investment in a bachelor's degree creates latent value that might never be translated into cash flow in the form of salary increases. Some translation from asset to income is an important action required for the corporation to benefit from the original investment as is shown in chapter 6. The concept of switching costs, to be discussed in appendix C, is important to understanding the behavioral aspects of the incongruity between asset value and income stream. Switching costs are the economic variable that blocks full market translation of assets into full cash income for the employee.

Barrier 3: The Employee Coinvestment Cost Is too High

As was seen in the earlier chapter, cash investment in earning a degree is only one component of the total investment. In addition to cash, the employee must also be willing to invest his or her time and psychic energy. If one is a young mother, time is already a precious personal resource, as is her energy level. By the time she puts in a full day at the office, takes care of the kids and has a little time to relax, the time required to study is a very scarce personal resource indeed. In our modern fast-paced world, time may be a more precious resource than money for the young professional.

The attractive employee ROI is clear evidence as to why employees find tuition reimbursement an attractive benefit when considering a new employment offer. Indeed, for those corporate benefit departments generally chartered to administer it, tuition reimbursement is most often viewed as a recruiting instrument, not as an investment resource to enhance existing asset value. The implications for the other half of the human asset equation, retention, are examined in chapter 6.

5 Tuition Reimbursement
Myths vs. Reality

In a world of continuous change it is an implicit assumption of every organization that continuous reinvestment in employee know-how is required to remain competitive. The challenge lies in bridging the gap between realizing the importance of developing new knowledge and skills and actually allocating investment capital to create them. Some corporate cultures foster the view that the original hire was done to recruit new knowledge and skills. Unfortunately, like depreciation in a plant and the equipment, education and skills are becoming obsolete as new knowledge is being created at an ever more rapid pace. In addition, it is often viewed that education benefits the employee more than it benefits the company. Later calculations will demonstrate that this is, in fact, true. Nonetheless, the reality of human behavior is that the employees are motivated to seek education independent of the priorities of the company.

"Of all the forms of company-sponsored development, college courses covered by tuition reimbursement are most likely to be seen by employees as providing marketable skills, because of the broad content and qualifications they offer."[41] "Seventy-five percent of U.S. establishments with more than twenty employees and almost all large employers offered some type of reimbursement benefit."[42] From a financial consideration, this corporate resource totals more than $10 billion of corporate investment made annually by

U.S. corporations. Yet only 2 percent of companies track the ROI of an employee's continuing education.[43]

There are a number of management myths related to corporate investment in degree programs for employees. Four of these myths and the data to refute them are provided here for discussions with the CEO.

Myth 1

"Why should I pay to help my employees get degrees? They will just leave the company when they graduate."—senior management

Analysis: This myth is largely based on the obvious conclusion that getting a degree is of considerable value to the employee. We have already confirmed this to be true in analysis presented earlier. Table 4.2 documents the extremely attractive financial returns to employees. The mathematics supports the intuition that is the basis for the concern. But attractive financial returns are not the only issue in play here. The Benson et al research shows that taking courses and receiving a bachelor's degree actually reduced turnover by 55 percent in the studied company where salary actions were related to the awarding of the degree.[44] This result is consistent with findings in retention surveys that list the opportunity to develop and grow as one of the most attractive benefits of a job. This refutes the myth, because the data shows increased retention and not greater turnover when policies include salary action and promotion as part of the investment strategy. The truth in this study is exactly the opposite of the myth.

Myth 2

"If I want employees who have a bachelor's degree, I am better off hiring them from outside rather than developing them from within."—senior executives and HR managers

Analysis: This myth is closely linked to Myth 1 and is amplified by the implicit assumption that somehow a new employee with experience is more valuable than a current employee. This is a form of the "grass is greener on the other side" philosophy. There is also an implicit assumption that somehow the company recruiting is avoiding the investment required to acquire the degree by recruiting individuals who already have the degree. In the case of degree holders in the marketplace, it is a fact that someone other than the company has made the education investment. Although the hope is for a free lunch, the hiring company is going to pay the full market value of that asset. That market value incorporates into the market price the cost of the investment to get the degree (see table 4.1). As a result of employee switching costs (see appendix C), it is almost always the case that it is more economical to invest in the new skills for current employees than to hire those skills on the open market. Financial defense of this conclusion is presented in chapter 9.

Myth 3
"Why should I pay to help my employees take courses of their own choosing? They'll just take courses that they like, courses like art, or psychology, or basket weaving, or travel—courses that they might enjoy, but that have no value to the company."—senior executives, CFOs and HR managers

Analysis: It is true that, under current "benign neglect" policy administration of tuition reimbursement resources, employees are largely given free rein to choose whatever curriculum they want to take, subject to approval from their supervisors. In reality, the supervisor oversight is loosely administered with very little actual controls as to the strategic relevance of the specific education investment. Data show that although this is the practical reality, employees are strongly motivated to make education choices that enhance their own value to their current employer. Indeed, in 85 percent of the cases where adult learners seek education, their decision is driven by career transition issues.[45] It is logical that targeting their educational investment in areas that have the potential for career advancement with their current employer will be the preferred educational choice. Indeed, in the Benson et al research, analysis of the education choices revealed that only 7.3 percent of the degree activity was not in some way related to the business objectives of the corporation. Conversely, more than 90 percent of the tuition reimbursement resources were being used to develop skills that related to the corporation's business.

Myth 4

"The whole ROI concept in human capital is bogus. Since it can't be measured anyhow, I am simply going to view it as a current period cost and not as an investment at all. So don't even try to increase the budget for tuition reimbursement or training."—senior executive

Analysis: There is considerable contention over the issue of ROI within the training and education departments of corporations. The training profession itself has people who debunk the very concept of ROI in human capital investments. The session "The Myth of Training ROI," which was held at the Training 2004 Conference Expo March 1-3, 2004, actually argued that it is impossible to view human capital as an asset and expenditures related to improve human capital as an investment.[46] The reality is that the HR profession must build a credible case for objective measurement of ROI to fulfill the senior executive demands for strategic investment in human capital. There is no credible alternative to ROI.

Strategic investment in human capital involves a number of administrative and management issues that need to be addressed. These include the following:

- ▶ What should the annual budget be for investment in human capital?
- ▶ What should the policy be with regard to the qualification and timing of the tuition reimbursement benefit?
  - ▶ What courses (degrees) should qualify for reimbursement?
  - ▶ When should the reimbursement take place?
  - ▶ How should the policy be administered to minimize administrative overhead costs?
- ▶ Should tuition reimbursement cover 100 percent of the costs or should there be some cost sharing or cap on total expenditures?
- ▶ What are the ROI implications from the interaction between the tuition reimbursement policy, salary actions and promotion?

These and other policy and administration issues are addressed in the chapters that follow.

6 The Value of Developing Skills in a Global Economy

Retirement, voluntary turnover, growth, new market opportunities, new technology, changing customer demands are only a few of the external forces driving the need to invest in human capital. McKinsey and Co. has characterized the future as the era of extreme competition.[47] A company has only two options for securing the human capital required to compete in the emerging global economy. The corporation can either *invest* in training and education to develop new capabilities in its existing employees, or it can *recruit* the required skills on the open market. In the language of the industrial age, it is a make vs. buy decision. In the age of human capital, the choice is to develop or recruit. The challenge is to make decisions that produce the best ROI.

Virtually every major U.S. corporation has a tuition reimbursement benefit as part of its compensation package. Whether or not to offer the benefit is no longer an option in the marketplace for human capital. Failure to offer the benefit would put the organization at a distinct recruiting disadvantage. The irony is that the corporate resource most important for developing employees is most often discussed relative to recruiting—procuring human capital resources from outside of the company.

The challenge is to deploy management policies, practices and procedures that improve the financial return.

Only after the parameters have been defined is analysis of policy options and program impact possible.

Several of the key parameters have already been identified earlier in this book. These include the objective market value of the bachelor's and master's degrees. The corporate ROI calculation requires the examination of several additional parameters, including the market interest rate, the tuition cost of securing a bachelor's or master's degree, incremental recruiting costs and, importantly, the retention rate or one minus the turnover rate. In all of the discussion that follows, objective measures of the average value of these key parameters are used to validate the structure of the corporate ROI model.

The numerical values derived in these analyses are based on national averages and specific parameter values documented and referenced from quantitative research. In all cases, the specific ROI for any particular corporation depends upon the unique value of the parameters for that company. This makes measurement of the specific values of the critical parameters mandatory for the specific corporation. The first step in every application has to be the determination of the parameter values in the application. Experimentation and evaluation then follow as policies are tested and their financial impact evaluated.

Let us examine the question at the individual employee level and then extend the analysis to the organization as a whole. In the recruiting decision to hire a new employee with the required skills represented by a bachelor's degree, the company will pay, on average, $51,194 (2002 data) in annual salary (see table 4.1). In addition, the corporation will incur out-of-pocket recruiting costs including administrative overhead, interview time, lost productivity, and relocation costs, to name a few.

It is the inclusion or exclusion of some or all of these associated parameters that often produces the tremendous variability in HR estimates of personnel replacement costs. The financial implications of these costs are examined in detail in chapter 9. For now, only out-of-pocket costs considered in the analysis are the same ones used in the employee ROI analysis, namely, the difference between the average salary for a bachelor's degree holder and the average salary for a non-degree holder.

As with the earlier disclaimer, there is a second disclaimer I wish to advance at this juncture in anticipation of the inevitable and healthy debate to follow. All of the parameters within a company have a *distribution* of values. The model is built on average values. The implications of this can be seen by examining the variability in individual performance. "The rule of thumb is that top performers outperform average performers by 40 to 50 percent."[48] McKinsey and Co. estimates the variance to be even higher. "Highly talented managers are 50 percent to 130 percent more productive than average and low-performing managers."[49] Here again, the analysis is on the average and does not attempt to evaluate the financial impact of variability over the entire distribution. Expansion of the analysis to include the variability would be a valuable extension of the financial framework presented here.

One way to think about the tuition reimbursement benefit is to view it as a pool of investment capital available to the company to develop the same know-how otherwise recruited on the open market. Therefore, the financial return on the investment in an existing employee over the hiring of a new employee with comparable credentials is derived by the analysis of the financial implications of the develop vs. recruit decision. Extension of the results to the corporation as a whole provides the analysis for determining ROI on corporate-wide tuition reimbursement policy.

The increased asset value of the bachelor's degree awarded has a *defined* market value for the employee but only an *expected* value for the corporation. Important business factors define key parameters, which impact the actual value of the ROI to the corporation. The first two factors examined are the free will of the employee and the average salary increases awarded the employee in each of the years of the forecast period. We examine the latter first.

The corporation derives a *net* annual value increase equal to the prorated asset value increase, minus the increased incremental annual salary raise related to the awarding of the degree. In the Benson et al research, the annual increment of salary increase for degree awardees is $1,198 per year.[50] That is, on average, employees awarded a bachelor's degree under the corporation's tuition reimbursement policy received annual salary increases $1,198 per year *greater* than the salary increases awarded employees not taking advantage of the tuition benefit. In effect, the financial impact is that the corporation is decreasing the increased asset value to the corporation by the sum of $1,198 each year, through cash distribution to the employee receiving the degree. The net asset value adjusted for the cash distribution is called the corporate net value in this analysis.

The second adjustment results from modeling the impact of free will. Once the employee has received a bachelor's degree, the future net value of the asset is available to the benefit of the corporation only if the employee actually remains employed by the company making the human capital investment. The following formula is the probability that the employee is still employed by the investing corporation in year t after degree award:

$$(1\text{-turnover})^t \qquad t = 1, 2, \ldots, 10$$

The formula that describes the base case and the data for the Corporate ROI is stated in appendix A. With a reimbursement policy of 100% company paid tuition distributed at the beginning of the period, the expected ROI to the corporation is:

$$ROI = 71\%$$

Two additional operating factors warrant examination of this critical ROI calculation. One of the conclusions of the Benson et al research is that the awarding of a bachelor's degree when combined with salary actions reduces the turnover of those employees receiving the bachelor's degree by 55 percent. Given this adjustment, this is the turnover parameter in the appendix A calculation:

$$.144 \times (1\text{-}55\%) = .0648$$

This favorable impact from the degree award alters the expected ROI to the corporation to an adjusted value ROI_a

$$ROI_a = 124\%$$

This ROI calculation shows an ROI increase of 53 percentage points as a result of reduced turnover related to the taking of accredited courses and the awarding of bachelor's degrees. The calculation quantifies the important conclusion that retention is a very important parameter to the corporation in human capital investment. Nonetheless, the majority of companies surveyed (57 percent) *never* or *rarely* measures the impact of education and training investments on turnover or retention.[51]

Combinations of salary actions, retention rates, and tuition reimbursement policies create a near infinite number of ROI values that must be analyzed by each individual company. It is revealing to examine one more of these combinations where the 55 percent improvement in retention and a tuition reimbursement policy of 80 percent corporate and 20 percent employee interact. Call this value ROI_{aa}.

$$ROI_{aa} = 155\%$$

The financial impact of other policy options is examined in more detail in later chapters. What is clear at this point is that it is financially attractive for the corporation to invest in employees even in the face of the risks resulting from employee free will. The ROI calculation provides executives with the financial model to evaluate and track the fiscal impact of various human capital investment policies and related personnel decisions. Given that investment in human capital produces very attractive financial returns, the challenge becomes one of budgeting for maximum financial impact. The challenge is to determine how large the corporate budget for tuition reimbursement should be in any given year. This question is examined in detail in chapter 9.

7 Risk Management and Incentives for Improved Retention

Tuition reimbursement payment distributed to the employee upon completion of courses is not the only policy option to manage the tuition reimbursement resources of the corporation. Several policy alternatives increase the ROI while reducing the risk that results from an employee's free will. For the corporation, risk management is as important, if not more important than pure financial return. In absence of rigorous ROI measurement, uncertainty is actually the dominant consideration. It is largely the uncertainty associated with the employee's free will that keeps senior management and the benefits staff from aggressively promoting the use of tuition reimbursement as a strategic corporate resource. To become a strategic corporate resource, management has to be able to convert uncertainty into manageable risk.

To this point, the tuition reimbursement policy assumed in the calculations (with the exception of table 4.2) is the one most commonly used by companies today. That is the policy of distributing tuition reimbursement funds to the employee upon completion of each individual course. This minimizes the risk to the employee, but it creates maximum risk to the company as a result of the uncertainty resulting from free will.

Timing of tuition reimbursement distribution and the employee qualifications for payment are important for managing corporate risk. The potential negative impact of delayed benefit distribution is the possibility of reducing employee motivation. By dealing with the risk issues, the corporation has new communication options to motivate the employee. These options are explored in chapter 10.

In an alternative policy to distribution at the end of an individual course, the corporation should be considering delayed distribution. At a minimum, the corporation should be considering that the first distribution be made at the first anniversary of the completion of course work, with the second distribution occurring at the second anniversary of the same date. Under such a policy, full-time employment at the anniversary distribution dates is required to qualify for distribution.

This shift in policy has a risk/reward impact for the employee and the organization under *all* free will scenarios. In a modification of this delayed repayment to motivate securing of a degree—as opposed to simply taking individual courses, the distribution can be specifically linked to the awarding of a degree. Here, the awarding of the degree triggers distribution of the tuition reimbursement funds, and actual cash distribution takes place on the first and second anniversary of the degree award. There is a related cash flow effect of the policy for the employee. The carrot of two equal $8,640 distributions on the first and second anniversary dates operates very similar to a cash retention bonus. The important point here is that neither of the alternate tuition reimbursement policies reduces the ROI to the employee to an unattractive level. In both cases, the ROI to the employee remains well above 400 percent. Under this alternative, an employee who stayed with the company only until he obtained his degree and then immediately left for another company would have the base ROI of more than 400 percent, while a second employee who earned the degree and stayed with the firm the full reimbursement period has a considerably higher ROI.

The corporate risk implications of the delayed distribution are examined in table 7.1. In that analysis, the interaction between the employee risk/reward and the corporate risk/reward are shown side by side under the scenario that the employee departs as soon as they get their degree—the fear factor of Myth 1.

Table 7.1
Risk/Reward

Employee departs upon completion of degree but before the first anniversary

Employee		Corporation	
Cost	ROI	Cost	ROI
$17,280	400+%	$0	Minimum 0*

* Note: On an individual basis, the company does not get the multiyear return from the newly created asset. However, it does benefit from the three years of retention while the employee remains at the company while they are earning their degree.

The policy significantly alters the risk/reward equation for the corporation. This is especially important for corporations to fully and aggressively deploy their available tuition reimbursement resources. Understanding the financial implications of the risk is a necessary prerequisite to innovation. This is especially important because HR departments are notable for their conservative approach to risk and innovation in general. Indeed, it can be argued that experimentation and innovation is exactly what the CEO is asking from the HR department.

The cash flow and ROI for the corporation are shown in table 7.2 below.

Table 7.2
Tuition Reimbursement Policy
100% Reimbursement Benefit

	Concurrent	Two-year anniversary after degree
Corporate Cash distribution	$17,280	$13,727
Expected value Corporate ROI	71%	115%

The significant increase in the corporate ROI results largely from the fact that the corporation does not pay an employee before there is an opportunity for it to actually earn a return on the educational investment. In other words, the company avoids actually paying those employees who get their degree and immediately leave for employment elsewhere. This latter scenario is one of the major factors that preclude many organizations from aggressively promoting the tuition reimbursement benefit to current employees.

A natural skepticism must accompany this dramatic increase in the financial attractiveness for the corporation. Almost doubling the ROI looks like a free lunch. The implications can best be understood through an examination of the behaviors and motivations of the employee in combination with the extremely favorable ROI for the employee.

The calculations in chapter 4 show that the investment in a bachelor's degree is extremely attractive, even if the employee makes the entire investment out of his own personal capital (zero corporate tuition reimbursement). Under the extreme case when the employee fully funds his own education, the expected ROI to the employee is well over 400 percent. The employee incurs no greater personal risk under a corporate shift from a corporate tuition reimbursement policy of concurrent 100 percent reimbursement to the two-year anniversary policy. Even the magnitude of the employee ROI remains largely unaltered over time. The only employee impact occurs in the case where the employee exercises the free will option before the anniversary dates. With those employees who actually intend and indeed do stay with the company through the second anniversary, the actual numerator of the employee ROI is decreased only by the accumulated student loan interest over the period.

Examination of the potential motives of the employee is further revealing. If, at the beginning of the education investment activity, the employee is motivated to get his bachelor's degree for the purposes of immediately translating the increased asset value into actual personal cash flow—i.e., cashing in on the investment—he is free to do so. It is the potential that this employee intent actually exists that is the root of Myth 1. The actual intent of such an employee cannot be predetermined by the corporation and may not even be fully developed on the part of the individual when he begins his courses. Yet it is the *possible* existence of such intent that severely restricts many corporations from aggressively using tuition reimbursement resources for strategic human capital investment. Under the two-year anniversary policy, understanding the motivation and intent of the employee is not necessary for attractive risk/reward balance for both the employee and the corporation.

Most importantly, mitigating the risks that result from employee intent further empowers the corporation to favorably affect business outcomes. Current benign neglect tuition reimbursement policies remove one of the most important options for strategic human capital investment, namely, the corporation's active encouragement for employees to make the coinvestment that is of greatest benefit to the company. Today, few corporations actively encourage employees to coinvest in education aligned with business goals. One corporation that I know of personally that gets it right is First Data Corporation (FDC).

In conjunction with Bellevue University, FDC operating managers have been highly proactive at implementing a strategic alliance with the university to develop and deploy bachelor's degree completion programs aligned with the business objectives of the company. The alliance uses the elements of the university's Impact Partners program (see appendix D) to deploy degree-seeking programs that qualify for the corporation's tuition reimbursement benefit. By actively promoting the programs to employees, FDC has been able to rapidly accelerate its human assets in those technology skills needed to serve changing market conditions in the company's core credit card transactions processing business.

As with all significant change, the new policies have resulted in a degree of organizational trauma. In the FDC case, those staff personnel charged with controlling the level of tuition reimbursement expenditures have been in extended discussions with the operating personnel to understand the business impact of the corporate cash being invested. To the credit of the leaders of FDC, the business impact rationale has won the day. The outcome is that FDC has implemented human capital investment policies that link tuition reimbursement benefits to its business strategy.

The active role of the corporation is essential in shaping a true human capital investment strategy. Strategic management of the tuition reimbursement resources requires a far more proactive corporate approach than is being used under the policy of benign neglect. It is to the significant advantage of the corporation to actively promote education that supports business objectives. Such a posture has the side benefit of positioning the company as a learning organization—an important and attractive market position for recruiting, which is the other half of the human capital equation.

The corporation has strong incentives to communicate its vision for current and future skill needs to the employees. This is exactly the opposite of the widely used approach of keeping such information out of general corporate conversations for fear that employees might find the tuition reimbursement benefit even more appealing. Today, often it is the case that the last thing the HR manager wants is a spike in tuition reimbursement use when the corporation is charging that benefit as a current period expense, reducing current quarter earnings statements. Nothing is more likely to produce a call from the CEO's office than a unexpected negative impact on reported earnings. Operating within a budget is the way to make sure future expenditures are not unexpected.

The company should be encouraging the employee to invest in themselves in those areas known by the company to be of future value in its markets. This requires an aggressive use of the growing liquid capital of the corporation to develop those skills. It also requires an aggressive and proactive marketing campaign to the employees.

There are two related policy issues that are important to examine. They are turnover in raw form and administrative costs. The rapid changes in markets resulting from global competition and information technology are forcing organizations to constantly assess the new skills required to compete. The result is rapid change in the composition of the organization. For example, an organization with the average national turnover rate of 14.4 percent has a half life of a little over four years, where half life is the period of time it takes for one-half of the organization to be completely replaced. This places tremendous pressure on the organization, particularly when it comes to continuity of culture, vision, and the informal organizational networks required to compete in the modern economy.

It is little wonder that a common plea from corporate leaders is to find solutions to the rapid changes in their operating environments. While companies are simultaneously terminating large blocks of employees for cost or skill deficiency reasons, they are concurrently hiring new employees to acquire needed skills. The result is high turnover, a key parameter earlier defined as critical to the corporate ROI on human capital investment. It also has a significant negative impact on culture and the tacit knowledge of the organization, both important assets in the new global economy where experimentation and innovation are so important.

McKinsey and Co. characterizes this competitive environment as one of extreme competition. The recommended response is a wider and more urgent discussion of uncertainty and available options.[52] To create such a culture, informal networks and trust are prerequisites to innovation in the face of the increased uncertainty.

Many corporations are concerned about the administrative overhead costs of alternate tuition reimbursement policies. Most attempts to hold the employee financially responsible for continued employment related to tuition reimbursement have used the concurrent funds distribution with a signed agreement for the employee to repay in the event of his resignation. This creates the need for the company to chase the employee, creating administrative expenses for a collections activity. As a result, even among companies that require the signed obligation of the employee to repay upon resignation, some do not bother to actually go after the departed employee for repayment. One option actually reduces administrative overhead costs. The policy recommended is for the employee to contract directly with the university for courses and degree programs. Such an employee-university contract is a standard administrative procedure used by some universities specializing in serving adult learners. A contract between the employee and the university, along with actual attendance, qualifies the employee for a private loan or a U.S. Department of Education backed student loan, financed at very favorable terms. In the case of a Title IV student loan, the length of the loan is ten years at 3.37 percent annual interest through loans guaranteed by the DOE. Repayment of these loans begins six months after degree curriculum is completed.[53] These terms remove cash availability constraints from the employee independent of the specific corporate tuition reimbursement policy.

Although there are a large number of policy combinations for consideration, the final policy examined here is a multiyear payback schedule. Currently, the single-year expensing policy charges the current year with the maximum annual tuition reimbursement benefit for that year. Thus, for example, even if the employee invested in $10,000 worth of education in a given year, a $5,250 per year tuition reimbursement policy would cap the payment to the employee at the $5,250 mark, leaving the balance of $4,750 for the employee to pay out of his own pocket. An alternative policy is to agree to pay the employee up to $5,250 each year against the accumulated balance of all incurred educational expenses until such time as those balances are reduced to zero.

The importance of this policy option is not that the employee finds their own ROI so much more attractive. We have already seen in chapter 5 that the employee has ample ROI investment incentive under all tuition reimbursement policies, but that the future year benefit payment stream has the potential to be a strong retention factor, thus improving the corporate ROI. This may be a particularly important policy to consider in organizations with very high turnover.

The bottom line on tuition reimbursement policy is that there is a better set of options that alter corporate ROI while reducing the risk of the free will component. These outcomes have an impact on yield and participation, both important parameters in budgets for human capital investments.

8 Making the Case for Human Capital Investment to the CEO

The CEO is looking for the integration of the HR function with the CFO. Human capital measurements are required to deal with the majority of the company's valuation that has moved off of the accountant's balance sheet. At this point, the CFO is every bit as frustrated with the state of affairs as everyone else in the room. The accounting rules of the industrial age no longer provide the rigor and insight needed to preserve the historically close relationship with the CEO, the board of directors, and the stockholders. Corporate testimonies to the importance of people abound, as in "people are our most important asset." However, aside from making this statement, few companies report anything to demonstrate that this asset has an impact on the value of the enterprise. Research studies have revealed that even "best practice" companies report only a handful of people-related statistics in their public disclosures.[54]

The HR literature reflects the profession's search for solutions. "The problem may well be in the area of measurement—proving with data that the HR department is adding value."[55]

The real fear is that the HR department will lose its place at the table altogether. As distasteful as fielding the challenges hurled by the CFO may be, the prospect of not even being invited to the CEO discussion is worse.

HR literature such as the journal *Human Resource Planning* states the challenge. "If HR does not force its way

51

into the heart of strategic planning in organizations, it will default to a technical and transactional dead end. Upper management in most organizations is finally willing to recast HR into a role as equal business partner, but HR managers have to be willing and able to step up to that bigger role. There is a seat at the table. Is that seat going to be filled by an HR pro or someone else?"[56]

It's not that the CFO is insensitive to the human capital agenda. Thirty-nine percent of respondents in a CFO Research Services (www.cforesearch.com) survey, analyzed by Mercer Human Resource Consulting (www.mercerHR.com/CFO study), said they view human capital as an important driver of shareholder value. CFOs uniformly rank talent identification and organizational development as their top agenda areas. Robert J. Darretta, CFO at Johnson and Johnson, for example, considers "people development" his number one focus and Robert L. Lumpkins of Cargill states that CFOs need to be leaders with a mind-set that focuses on continuous improvement and talent management.[57] Yet, although on average companies spend over 30 percent of their revenues on salaries and benefits, only 16 percent indicate they have anything more than a moderate understanding of the return on those human capital investments.[58]

Even the CFO agrees that people are an important part of the performance of the company (92 percent said the workforce had a great effect on the ability to achieve customer satisfaction, 82 percent on profitability, and 72 percent on innovation and new product development), but there just wasn't any collective agreement on how to quantify this value. Most people in the study would like to measure human capital ROI—they just weren't sure how to do it.[59]

This brings us back to the basic challenge, which is to create the measurements that are acceptable to the CEO and the CFO. The foundation of the analysis is rooted in the capital investment approach where this particular part of the inquiry begins. We have already examined and integrated aspects of tangible asset capital investments including multi-period analysis, the time value of money and market-based asset valuation. What is needed now is the inquiry into what else capital investment accounting rules can contribute to human capital investment decisions.

Let's look at the basic parameters used in a typical multimillion dollar (assume $15 million) equipment investment. In this case, the business goals are to add output capacity to grow sales and increase productivity from equipment designed to deliver the best and latest efficiencies. In the broadest sense, investments in human capital are made for the same business reasons.

To begin with, in capital equipment decisions the operating manager responsible for producing the goods and services that generate revenue and profits would never say, "Oh, I don't know what I need, just send me whatever my employees pick for themselves" (benign neglect). In a widget company, the operating managers know they need assets that produce widgets. Widgets are what customers buy. Furthermore, these same operating managers will not accept just any new widget-making hardware. They need widget equipment that can produce widgets based on the latest technology because they know that if such technology exists, their competitors will be looking at it to gain a competitive advantage. The competitive dynamics of human capital investment are no different.

Yet, in the realm of benign neglect tuition reimbursement policies, the know-how the individual employee secures with his degree has little more than a random chance of actually aligning with the company's future business goals. Granted, the specificity of human knowledge is only a fraction of the specificity of a widget machine. The industrial era has the advantages of centuries of previous experience. Nonetheless, the challenge to define what is actually required as outputs of human capital investments remains every bit as important to the value of the investment as the outputs of the tangible asset investments are to the industrial age. The challenge is to move beyond the conceptual framework advanced in so much of the HR literature.

So what are activities the organization engages in to support the equipment investment decision? With a fifteen million dollar equipment investment, the organization is likely to commit several thousand person hours to produce engineering, manufacturing engineering, plant design, plant layout, vendor evaluation, and financial analyses. That data is needed to measure the parameters required for making the ROI calculation, which all companies require to justify the $15 million investment. The costs of these support activities to create the rigorous parameters for the business decision might total as much as 15 percent of the total project cost. In this fictitious example, that figure is $2.25 million of the entire $15 million project. The point is that investment in the analysis—which is required to justify the ultimate investment decision—is a fundamental prerequisite to the precision demanded by the CEO and the board of directors.

I am not aware of a single HR department that invests comparable resources to get the data required to support the $10 billion aggregated in tuition reimbursement investments. Creation of the critical data is a very important place to begin. Like the engineer responsible for the success of the $15 million equipment investment, the HR manager should be representing to the CEO and the CFO that the measurement of the key ROI parameters is a prerequisite to successful human capital investment. Investment in the data gathering is mandatory.

The budget is the starting point. It is the one universal component of every asset-based capital investment decision. Without a budget and a plan, human capital investment decisions rest on a bed of quicksand, subjecting them to the arbitrary and somewhat capricious decisions to cut expenditures as soon as the operating environment gets a little tough. The result puts the executive leadership in exactly the same place—namely far from a strategic human capital investment process. This is not a very comfortable place to be in a world of rapid and unpredictable change.

Human Capital Budgeting

One of the first observations about the budgeting of human capital investment is that most corporations don't do it. McKinsey and Co. found that "only 18 percent of the corporate offices we surveyed strongly agree that our annual talent review process has the same intensity and importance as the financial budget process."[60] Cox Communications CEO Jim Robbins made the same point in saying, "We spend four months per year on the (financial) budget process, but we hardly spend any time talking about our talent . . ."[61] I might add that the very absence of a human capital budgeting process is one of the reasons top management spends so little time on human capital investment decision making. If such a budget process did exist, it would help the CEO manage the *how* of human capital investment.

Under benign neglect human capital investment policies, the term budget is close to the *Compact Oxford English Dictionary* definition:

> Definition of *budget*: The amount of money needed or available for a purpose.[62]

The important part of this definition is "available for a purpose." When tuition reimbursement is booked as a current period expense, the total expenditure level is monitored in order to determine when the actual expenditure level reaches the level *available for a purpose*. Most often, the level *available for a purpose* is determined relative to the previous year's expenditure level.

The management challenge is to determine if this is the definition of budget being used by the organization in practice. If management discussions about the budget for human capital investment focus on previous year expenditures, then the definition applies. If these management discussions involve mostly caps, limitations, and controls rather than outcomes, then the definition applies. If management discussions are loaded with verbs that are in the past tense, then the definition applies. Another clue in the management discussion is whether the language of investment outcomes is absent. In contrast, outcomes are never absent in the CFO and operating manager discussions of capital investment budgeting.

The danger in the benign neglect approach is that the organization is looking backward, not forward. A backward perspective has virtually nothing to do with investment (see earlier definition) or strategy. It is a bit like driving a car by looking in the rearview mirror. Such a management approach has more to do with compliance and control than producing future business outcomes.

An alternate definition of budget from *Cambridge Dictionary of American English* more directly describes a future orientation to human capital investment advocated in this analysis.

> Definition of *budget*: to plan to spend (money) for a particular purpose.[63]

In this definition, the concept of a plan with implications for future periods of time and the link to a particular purpose, are important. The verb tense is future. The www.dictionary. com definition has a similar future orientation with the phrase, "intended expenditures for a given period."[64] Both *intended* and *plan* are significant departures from *available*. The challenge is to define a plan and to analyze the implications. These are precisely the goals of this chapter.

As noted, tuition reimbursement expenditures have been managed as a period cost. Although the level of expenditure is the key parameter being controlled, it is most often done through benchmarking relative to previous year expenditures. That is, the implicit budget is not a planning document to manage, but a control tool with little or no connection to strategic business objectives, market conditions or specific skill requirements for the coming years. These are all elements presented earlier as important components of tangible asset capital investment decision making. The analysis here looks forward. Several new management parameters are defined, including participation and yield.

To examine the budgeting question in human capital investments, it is necessary to create a context for such decisions. Business goals and financial measurements affect the definition of the parameters. Here we examine the XYZ Corporation with key parameters set at averages for American industry.

Table 9.1 The XYZ Corporation	
Total sales (billions)	$4.167
Sales per employee	$200,000
Average administrative cost per new hire	$10,057
Total employment	20,835
Total managers (20% of total)	4,167
Education mix % of total bachelor's holders	26.0%
Turnover (% per year)	14.4%
Note: Turnover new manager hires from *The War for Talent*	30.0%

The human capital investment strategy for the XYZ Corporation must deal with the need to replace 600 managers every year at the national average turnover rate of 14.4 percent per year. As discussed, the options are to recruit the replacement talent or to develop the talent from within. It is

assumed that the holding of a bachelor's degree is the prerequisite for being a candidate for a management position
at the XYZ Corporation. It is further assumed for comparison, that under "hire all new managers," that the policy has
been in place for years and 30 percent turnover applies.

Hire All New Managers (Recruit)

Given the turnover among new hires is 15.6 percentage
points higher than the turnover rate for the company
(nation), 1,250 managers must be hired each year.

Administrative costs to hire 1,250 managers:

$$1,250 \times \$10,057 = \$12,571,250.$$

New managers hired at market salary for bachelor's degree
holder.

Invest in Existing Employees (Develop):

The strategy in the example assumes new hires are recruited
without a degree at the entry level and that managers are
then developed internally through education to a bachelor's
degree level. Implementation of the strategy defines key
operating parameters for management guidance, including
participation rate, yield, and the profile of the multiyear
budget structure required to implement the strategy.

Appendix B contains the budget formula as well as specific budget levels required to fulfill the strategy shown in
summary in table 9.2

Table 9.2
Enrollment and Budget

	Year			
	Begin	-2	-1	0
No. of students	958	820	1,522	2,123
No. of managers	0	0	0	601
Yield		0	0	28%
Budget ($millions)	—	$4.72	$8.77	$12.22

Note: Year zero is the plan target year when the "develop" strategy supplies all of the managers needed by the company in that year. The number of students in each year sustains the strategy in years beyond year zero, given no growth or change in the turnover rate.

Several implications are immediately clear. The shift from a pure recruit strategy not only requires an identifiable budget for the first year, it requires an 86 percent increase in the budget the second year and another 39 percent increase in the budget the third year to get a steady flow of newly developed managers in each year in the future. In light of the fact that most tuition reimbursement budgets are managed as a current year expenditure calculated after the fact, it is extremely unlikely that this sustainable plan is going to be implemented by the CEO in the absence of some very serious justification. The multiyear financial implications of doing or not doing this plan are required. Obviously, a mix of develop and recruit strategies will actually be deployed in practice. For analysis purposes, the model assumes a 100 percent develop strategy for simplicity. The general implications of the comparison between develop and recruit apply no matter what the actual mix is.

Before we proceed to the financial implications, it is worth examining the parameters the HR department needs to be held accountable for the implementation of the plan. This plan requires the following performance parameters:

Table 9.3
Key HR parameters for the XYZ Corporation

Participation:	12%
Yield:	28%

Where:
- Participation is the percentage of eligible employees enrolled in a degree seeking program in a given year.
- Yield is the percentage of qualified managers produced every year as a ratio to the total number of employees receiving tuition reimbursement in that year.

Hitting these targets requires active programs to influence employee behavior. To reach these goals, it is very likely that the HR department will have to promote the education programs to employees. This is an activity that is rarely done. Why is this the case?

Under the management approach where tuition reimbursement benefits are viewed as current period operating costs, senior level executive pressures—including those from the CFO and the CEO—are to control these costs, *especially with regard to changes year over year*. The last thing the HR manager wants to happen is for utilization of tuition reimbursement benefits to increase by anything approaching double digits, let alone more than 80 percent in the next year. As a result, the plans of action required to meeting participation and yield parameters simply do not exist.

There are two policy decisions that are important to examine.

1. The financial implications of a pure recruit vs. a pure develop strategy.

2. The strategic and financial implications of a fixed year-over-year budget.

Calculations in appendix B show that the sustained budget to implement a full develop strategy for the XYZ Corporation is $12.22 million a year. This represents a total just under 1 percent of XYZ payroll (assuming payroll is 30 percent of revenue). It is interesting to compare this with the American Society for Training and Development (ASTD) estimate that training expenditures by the ASTD BEST award winners in 2004 were 4.16 percent of payroll.[65] An immediate conclusion is that, although companies benchmark their training expenditures as a percent of payroll, few make the same calculation for tuition reimbursement. It is also important to note that the total cost of a full degree strategy for total management replacement is less than 25 percent of the resources allocated for training.

The ROI implications of the earlier chapters must be factored into the analysis at this point. We have already calculated that administrative costs to hire the needed managers with a bachelor's degree from outside of the company are approximately $12.3 million every year. These expenditures are pure costs—indeed these are current period expenses with no enduring investment value relative to the alternative of developing talent. In comparison, development of managers has an average ROI of 71 percent based on the most unfavorable tuition reimbursement policy analyzed as concurrent with 100 percent tuition reimbursement in table 7.2. The financial comparison is shown in table 9.4

Table 9.4
Financial Comparison: Pure Develop vs. Pure Recruit
14.4% Turnover
($ millions per year)

	Charge to Ops.	Incremental		
		ROI	Value	Net value
Recruit admin. costs	$12.3	0%	$0	($12.3)
Develop costs	$12.22	71%	$2.43*	$2.43

* Note: 71% ROI on the yield portion of the total current year education costs. In this example, yield = 28%

The conclusion is that the develop option has the potential to create $14.73 million of incremental value *every year* because the company must recruit or develop six hundred new managers based on annual turnover. To secure this benefit, a multiyear plan is required.

Table 9.5
Financial Comparison: Pure Develop vs. Pure Recruit
6.5% Turnover with education (down 55%)
($ millions)

	Charge to Ops.	Incremental		
		ROI	Value	Net value
Recruit admin. costs*	$12.3	0%	$0	($12.3)
Develop costs	$5.02	124%	$1.93**	$1.93
Cash saving	$7.28			

* Note: In pure recruit, turnover is still 14.4%

** Note: 124% ROI on the yield portion of the total current year education costs. In this example, yield = 31%

The second budget policy to be examined is that of constant tuition reimbursement budget each year. The fixed level is arbitrarily set at $5 million a year.

Table 9.6
Budget and Enrollment
Fixed annual tuition reimbursement budget: $5 million

	Year				
	Begin	-2	-1	0	+1
No. of students	1,014	868	868	868	868
Budget ($M)	—	$5	$5	$5	$5
Graduates	—	—	—	636	92
Participation		18%	18%	18%	18%
Yield	—	—	—	73.3%	10.6%

Conclusion: Fixed annual budgets lead to stable enrollment and fixed low participation, but the yield jumps around dramatically.

The implications are that the parameters of enrollment and fixed budget level are easy and convenient to manage, but they produce wildly swinging variation in the key outcome parameter that is the number of new managers created in each year.

Pure develop vs. pure recruit strategies are not the only options available to the company. In some circumstances, the decision might be to hire a certain percentage of managers from outside of the company to build new blood and infuse new ideas. GE regularly fills about 20 percent of top management positions from outside of the company each year.[66] The associated turnover in such an externally hired population is approximately 30 percent per year.[67] This higher turnover rate compares with the internal company turnover of 14.4 percent used in these analyses.

A strategic mix of develop vs. recruit will proportionally affect the values defined in tables 9.4 and 9.5 above. The main point is that the ratio of develop to recruit should be a strategic variable managed, not a dependent variable that falls out of policy decisions to stabilize current period tuition reimbursement expenditures under benign neglect policies.

For the constant expenditure case results of table 9.6, the annual requirement for 600 new managers swings from recruiting of zero percent in year zero to 85 percent the next year. This is hardly the stable 20 percent targeted by GE.

In summary, there is a compelling financial rationale for creating the human capital investment budget based upon the company's projected needs. This analysis has focused on the number of managers needed in the future. The analysis applies to any critical subpopulation of the company's human capital. As with the ROI calculations, the retention rate, or one minus the turnover rate, is a key variable to be managed by the HR department. What is new here is the ROI measurement that makes it possible to analyze the financial impact of various human capital investment decisions. In addition, the parameters of yield and participation relate much more directly to creation of future value than do stable enrollment levels and constant budgets.

10

Not All Human Capital Is the Same

Specific strategic issues examined in this chapter include variation between companies and the rationale for targeting human capital investment to subpopulations within the company. Current HR policies are largely managed as a monolithic company-wide benefit for all qualified employees.

As an anchor we begin with a definition.

Definition of *strategic*: forming part of a long-term plan or aim to achieve a specific purpose.[68]

This definition reinforces the importance of the multi-period analytical framework integral to tangible asset based capital investment decisions. Thus, the modifier *strategic* and the root *capital investment* form multiperiod bookends around the human element of human capital investment. The temporal framework further challenges the widely practiced management approach of booking training and education expenditures as current period costs. It is very difficult to conclude that the current period cost accounting is strategic in any fundamental way. A new paradigm is needed.

In human capital investment strategy, it is not so much the level of an *individual's* position that is most important to the human capital investment decisions. What is important is the *group* of skills, experience, and knowledge that is necessary to the success of the enterprise. Some classes of human capital are far more critical to the success of companies in one industry than the same skills are to the success of companies in another industry.

For example, high-caliber materials scientists, manufacturing engineers, and computer design engineers are absolutely essential to the survival of Intel. This same know-how has virtually no value to the business model used by Wal-Mart. And although highly educated chemists and physicists, many with multiple PhDs, are critical to the Battelle Institute (a high-technology research and consulting organization in Columbus, Ohio), that same human capital has virtually no role at a telemarketing company like West Corporation. For the latter, it is much more important to be able to develop and retain operating managers who can manage large groups of customer service representatives. When recruiting is employed to procure the needed skills, targeting is easily implemented. When benign neglect tuition reimbursement policies are used, targeting is much less effective, especially when the corporation fails to communicate information about what skills have future value to the enterprise.

The importance of these distinctions is not that they exist, but that the company needs to manage human capital investment policies that reflect the needs of that particular business. One size does not fit all. The practical question is, so what?

The ROI equations identify turnover as a key parameter in the ROI calculations. The level and criticality of turnover varies greatly between companies and between professional groups within companies. The turnover of high-powered PhDs is much different than the turnover rate of telemarketing agents, yet human capital investment decisions are required in both cases. Likewise, the availability and market salary of PhDs is vastly different than the value of the same parameters for telemarketing agents needed by West Corporation or checkout associates critical to Wal-Mart. The national average turnover rate of 14.4 percent is insufficiently precise to apply to both West Corporation and Battelle Institute. Each company needs to have its own data on each of its own key human capital groups.

Looming on the horizon of all of these human capital markets is the inevitability of the demographic trends. In the U.S., the baby boomers are going to retire in huge numbers in the next decade while the pool of qualified replacement workers is going to grow slowly at best. The supply is not encouraging. Since 1985, the total number of students enrolled in ninth through twelfth grades in U.S. public schools has only grown by a total of 14.6 percent in the thirteen years since 1985. The pipeline of candidates is much smaller than the demand for skills.[69]

The multiperiod aspect of strategic human capital investments has far greater significance in the case of highly educated physical scientists with PhDs or electronic chip designers with decades of practical experience. In these human capital domains, the investment cycle to develop those human assets is much longer than the investment cycle required to produce a high-performing telemarketing agent. The strategy of recruit instead of develop (see Myth 2), which has worked in recent decades, may in fact, be inadequate to produce the number of educated scientists and engineers needed in the very near future.

The implications extend beyond PhDs and electronic chip designers. The strategic generalization is that the very professional categories growing in importance as a result of information technology and global competition are the same categories that have longer human capital investment cycles. It is in these categories where the greatest management attention needs to be focused—where the strategic issues intersect with the multiperiod characteristics of investment decision making.

Distinctions between companies and industries have applicability to human capital investment within a given corporation. Currently, tuition reimbursement benefits are largely administered uniformly across all employment categories and employment levels. The specific purpose of many current tuition reimbursement benefit policies is to give equal opportunity to all employees, independent of level, external supply, or business criticality. It may be the case that a particular organization wishes to preserve this specific social welfare function for its policies. No matter what its social benefit, such uniform policies fail the test of being strategic human capital investments. Although the choice is certainly the prerogative of the organization, it is a choice that should be made explicitly, not implicitly. Too much is at stake.

So what would an alternative strategy for human capital investment look like if it were acknowledged that some positions and skills are more important than others, and as a result, warrant greater investment resources? Consideration of such an alternative has to include options that, at first, appear radical. If electronic chip engineers are more critical to the future success of the company than forklift drivers, the corporation should be developing more engineers than drivers. In terms of tuition reimbursement policy, this differentiation might be implemented by giving engineers (a class of employees) unlimited tuition reimbursement for graduate degrees (a class of investment) while limiting annual reimbursement for individual courses to $5,250 per year.

The Benson et al research reveals another important strategic dimension of managing tuition reimbursement policies. That research shows that both taking courses and receiving bachelor's degrees actually reduce the critical turnover parameter by roughly 55 percent where degree holders received higher salary increases on average.[70] Yet human capital investment in graduate degrees actually increases the critical turnover parameter by 27 percent when no promotion followed the awarding of the graduate degree.[71] The strategic implication is that career planning may not be so critical in the majority of the employee population, but it is extremely important in the employee population receiving graduate degrees. In the Benson et al research, failure to integrate employee succession planning with tuition reimbursement policies actually decreases the ROI on resources being expended. In that case, a tuition reimbursement policy intended to enhance the asset value to the company actually reduced it. The hidden costs are even greater.

Employees willing to invest the personal resources required to earn a graduate degree are some of the most talented and highly motivated employees in the organization. They also are the employees who have significant accumulated asset value because they already hold a bachelor's degree. Finally, these highly educated employees have a long investment cycle to develop their human asset value to the company. Demographics further compound the problem. At a minimum, the option to recruit replacement human assets will become more expensive over the next decade. The linking of tuition reimbursement with promotion is strategic. This is another example of why benign neglect is not strategic.

There is another dimension of policy refinement available to the company. Some individuals are more predisposed to be learners than others. Again, at the risk of being whistled out-of-bounds by advocates of social engineering, a debate about how to advise and counsel individual employees with regard to their education has the potential to be a strategic approach to human capital investment.

The Gallup Organization has a highly refined instrument titled SF[34] to identify an individual's top talents.

Based upon the statistical analysis of more than three million individuals, Gallup has identified thirty-four behavioral categories that define talents or what it calls strengths of human beings. Based upon online responses to one hundred and eighty questions, Gallup is able to provide any individual with a profile of the top five strengths of that individual. Several of those classifications identify a predisposition to learning. These include *input, ideation, intellection, and learner*.

Variable distribution of tuition reimbursement based on the Gallup strengths finder (SF) instrument is potentially in violation of existing equal opportunity laws. Nonetheless, there is nothing that precludes the corporation from using some of its own cash reserves to fund each employee's access to the Gallup SF[34] assessment instrument to provide every employee with important information about whether further education might leverage their personal strengths. Helping employees identify that they are high in *learner* and *input* strengths could be exactly the catalyst these high-potential employees need to make the coinvestment in education. The financial incentive is the increase in their asset value.

We have merely scratched the surface of strategic factors for consideration in the strategic human capital investment decisions. Management has two obvious opportunities. First, tuition reimbursement policies need to be examined relative to their strategic importance to the company's future. Not all human capital investments are equally critical and indeed may vary widely from company to company. Second, organizations need to begin to examine variable application of resources within the company based on business objectives.

What is eminently clear is that tuition reimbursement policies that look backward, are administered with benign neglect policies, and are uniform for all employees in all circumstances are not strategic. Just as in capital investment decision making, strategic human capital investments need to be targeted and focused to the benefit of the strategic outcomes for the organization in total.

11 The Bottom Line

Currently, tuition reimbursement resources are largely accounted for as current period costs. The management of this pool of more than $10 billion in corporate resources is largely ad hoc with very little top-level management focus other than to control costs. In this context, the CEO shares the CFO's low enthusiasm for spending much time considering any alternative to current policies. Meanwhile, the HR manager languishes on the outside of strategic decision making vital to defining the future success of the enterprise. For the HR department, annual budget reviews on the tuition reimbursement benefit are short, perfunctory discussions with the HR manager defending why the budget should not be cut.

One fundamental factor has changed from the industrial age. The fundamental change is that the impact of rigorous accounting tools used to guide the tangible asset capital investment decisions has been radically diminished in importance as a result of information technology and globalization. Where the capital assets of the corporation stated on the balance sheet accounted for 62 percent of the company's market value as recently as 1982, today the value is closer to 15 percent. Yet, the myths explored in chapter 5 currently block aggressive management actions to strategically manage human capital investment. The creation of a mathematically rigorous decision model opens the way to new management approaches.

All three of the main executive players in this drama are frustrated and concerned. As a response, some corporations have created a new senior executive level position titled chief learning officer (CLO). These newly created CLOs most often represent the interests of the HR department in human capital investment discussions with other senior level executives of the company.

The goal of this book is not to reject the disciplines of accounting but to learn from the lesson—to build upon the rigorous approach used in capital investment decision making. By building upon objective data and mathematical modeling, we have created a management framework for managing human capital investment decisions. The recommended approach moves from the single-period expenditure accounting to a multiperiod asset investment model. Of critical importance to the conclusions and implications is the explicit acknowledgement of the employee's free will. Without this conscious selection decision, migration to a multiperiod asset model is impossible.

In anticipation of the inevitable conversation with the CFO, subjective assignment of return values has been abandoned for objective data from multiple sources. The key concepts being advanced include a rigorous measurement of ROI, an elusive goal for the HR manager, the derivation of a human capital investment budget, and the framework for rigorous analysis of yet unexplored policy alternatives. In addition, valuable concepts including participation, yield, and switching costs have been introduced to assist in the management of corporate resources.

A road map for important human capital investment decisions has been defined. The individual company must have much better measurements on a defined set of key business parameters identified here. At a minimum, these include far better measurement of the level of investment (I), and refined data on the key parameter of turnover. As it turns out, turnover is central to both the measurement of ROI and the calculation of the budget. Accurate measurement of turnover among targeted subpopulations, such as engineers, scientists, key supervisors, and managers is important to understanding the financial implications of human capital investments in these subpopulations of employees.

In the end, this book is the intersection of human behavioral factors with the financial language and world-view of the CFO. It is at the intersection of the three-way conversation between the CFO, the HR manager and the CEO that the models converge. Neither the HR manager nor the CFO and CEO like the current state of uncertainty. The opportunity is to create future value from current period human capital investments. The challenge is to implement new policies and procedures to impact value in the market place.

Appendix A
ROI Model
Employee ROI

$$ROI\ (\%) = \{\{[\sum_{t=1}^{10} Ri_t \times (1/(1 + It))^t\ ]\ /\ \ (TT_p - I_c)\} - 1\} \times 100$$

Where:
- ► TT_p—program p total tuition cost to complete bachelor's degree ($)
- ► I_c—corporate tuition reimbursement contribution to degree in ($)

  $[TT_p > I_c]$ for mathematical consistency

- ► It—prevailing market interest rate (%)
- ► Ri_t—return to employee i in year t from increase in market value of asset in year t ($)

Note: The incremental value to employee i (Ri) is a function of the academic credits employee i brings to the investment. In all calculations it is assumed that the employee already has 60 credits toward the 127 credits required to earn the bachelor degree. Therefore, the ROI calculations cover the investment and incremental return related to the balance of 67 credits earned..

$$ROI\ (\%) = \{\{\sum_{t=1}^{10} [((Ri_t - (Si_t \times t)) \times (1/(1 + It))^t \times (1 - T)^t\ ]/I_c\} - 1\} \times 100$$

Corporate ROI
Where:
- ► I_c—corporate tuition reimbursement contribution to degree in ($) $[I_c > 0]$
- ► Si_t—The difference between the base salary and the new salary in period t for taking courses or getting a degree ($)

➤ It—prevailing market interest rate (%)

➤ T—annual company turnover rate (%)

Values Used in Body of Paper and Derivation of ROI Calculations

$TT_p = \$17,280$

> Note: degree completion tuition costs for student entering Bellevue University online accelerated bachelor's degree completion program with 60 transferable credits.

$Ri_t = \$12,615 \; t = 1, 2, \ldots, 10$

> Note: This is the incremental value of a bachelor's over no degree conservatively prorated over transferred credits $(\$51,194 - \$27,280)*(1-60/127)$

$Si_t = \$ 0$ in year t for employees not enrolled in any classes and $\$1,198$ per year for employees who earned a bachelor's degree at year t = -1: t = 1, 2, 3, . . ., 10

$It = 6\%$ per annum

$T = 14.4\%$ per year.

$I_c = \$17,280$ or 100% of total tuition program costs paid at time t = 0

> Note: In the employee return calculations, I_c is varied to calculate sensitivity. Corporate ROI calculations in the body I_c are equivalent to a 100% tuition reimbursement policy.

Appendix B
Human Capital Investment Budget

Business Goal: Replace from the total of M managers a year lost to turnover T with current employees educated with a bachelor's degree in management.

$$(1)\ S_k = \sum_{t=-2}^{k} (M \times T) \times (1 - T)^t \qquad k = -2, -1, 0$$

$$(2)\ B_k = C_p \times S_k$$

Where:

S_k = Number of employees enrolled at the end of year k (#)

B_k = Budget in year t to fill all vacated management positions each year in the future beginning in year t = 0 ($)

M = Total number of management positions in year t=0 (#)

C_p = Tuition for one year of bachelor's degree program p ($)

T = Management Turnover rate per year (%)

Assumptions:
- ▶ Employees begin degree completion program with 60 credits
- ▶ Course load requires three years to complete bachelor's degree
- ▶ Corporate tuition reimbursement policy distribution in year of course

Table B1
Enrollment and Budget—fully funded plan

Data for XYZ corporation:

$M = 4,174$
$T = 14.4\%$
$C_p = \$5,760$ per year

	Year			
	Begin	-2	-1	0
No. of students	958	820	1,522	2,123
Budget allocation ($M)	—	$4.72	$8.77	$12.22

Appendix C
Switching Costs

The concept of switching costs is well documented in technology markets. A discussion of the concept is a part of the battle between Linux and Microsoft as reported in the article "Linux, Inc," *Business Week*, January 31, 2005.[72] Software vendors are particularly attune to the economic implications. In technology applications, there are multi-year implications from an initial decision to use a particular set of software programs. Business processes get molded by and depend upon the structure and functionality of the software. Historical databases are built and maintained with the commands and functions of the installed systems. Probably the most insidious of all, behavioral patterns are formed at the level of the individual employee and become extremely difficult to change. The result is significant and growing switching costs not directly reflected in the purchase price of software. Indeed, many times the price of the new alternative is significantly below the out-of-pocket cost to maintain the current software.

Even in the face of direct cost-benefit comparisons, it is extremely difficult for the company to migrate to a new software platform. An analogous phenomenon exists in labor markets where employees have real switching costs to themselves and their families associated with changing employers. The case is made clear with the examination of a hypothetical 38-year-old married male professional with two children.

Before he was married, life for our hypothetical employee had few encumbrances. It is likely there were no mortgage payments, few possessions, and a limited set of community connections that at the beginning of his career, largely involved weekend golfing outings with his male buddies. Life was simple. All professional options were feasible, including geographic location. At that point in life, physical relocation involved little more than a moving truck rental for a weekend.

At thirty-eight years old, this same male has a very different set of variables to consider with the decision to maximize his cash return in the labor market. To begin with, he must consider the economic variables of selling a house, finding a new home, negotiating new contracts and possibly purchasing new furnishings as a condition for maintaining domestic tranquility. The non-economic barriers are probably even greater. One implication of this is that newly hired younger employees are likely to have significantly lower switching costs than more mature and established employees. This is no doubt true for both males and females. The related financial implication is that the financial risk of any tuition reimbursement policy resulting from free will is lower for the married thirty-eight-year-old employee vs. the single twenty-two-year-old employee.

For the thirty-eight-year-old employee, departure from his current employer involves the termination of relationships with a network of business associates and friends. In addition, over the years he has accumulated tacit knowledge about his employer's business model, developed key relationships, acquired knowledge about technology, processes and culture that, if not directly compensated for, reduce the stress from the unknown. His wife and children add to the switching costs.

Virtually every husband has faced the prospect of asking his spouse to give up the network of social and professional relationships she has worked so hard to build over the years. In a previous era, the request to relocate the family involved the severing of many of these cherished spousal investments in their life together.

To make matters even more complicated, in the majority of households the spouse has a career too. In over half of American homes, the spouse is also a professional with an investment in her current position. All of the psychological and economic costs that accrue to the male accrue equally if not more so to the female since she is not the one initiating the relocation discussion in this hypothetical example.

All this is to say nothing of the family cost involved in asking the two hypothetical teenage daughters to leave their high school friends to move out of state. Some of these relationship costs are never recovered inside of the family workings.

Actual switching costs are an important parameter. They are also measurable. The data group is the population of employees who voluntarily leave the company over a period of time. Obviously, the lower the observed switching cost for departing employees, the lower are those non-salary issues that are affecting retention.

While switching costs work to the benefit of the corporation with regard to the ROI from development, they work against the corporation when it comes to recruitment. Under the recruit option, the company is attempting to overcome the switching costs when hiring the new employee and may incur significant out-of-pocket incremental costs to do so.

Appendix D
Bellevue University IMPACT Partners Program

- Specification: Corporate account definition of skills, knowledge capability requirements
- Design: Educational Program elements—courses, learning, objectives, delivery mode, scheduling
- Marketing: Communication program to employees: Features, Benefits, Address concerns, Advising
- Delivery: Online Programs
- Return: Assessment of business impact/metrics for Employees & Managers

Notes

1. Butler, Patrick et al. 1997. "A Revolution in Interaction," McKinsey Quarterly 1: 8.
2. EXECSIGHT. (2004). *Transforming Corporate Leadership, Best Practices in Executive Education*. (Q1, 2004). [Whitepaper]. pg. 6.
3. Michaels, E., Handfield-Jones, H. & Axelrod, B. (2001). *The War For Talent*. McKinsey & Company, Inc. pg. 4.
4. Michaels, E., Handfield-Jones, H. & Axelrod, B. (2001). *The War For Talent*. McKinsey & Company, Inc. pg. 6.
5. Gale Group, Inc. (2004). "The Race for Talent: Retaining and Engaging Workers in the 21st Century." *Human Resource Planning Society*, September 1, 2004.
6. Weatherly, Leslie A. "The Value of People." *HRMagazine,* Alexandria: Sept. 2003. 48: Issue 9, pg. S1.
7. Michaels, E., Handfield-Jones, H. & Axelrod, B. (2001). *The War For Talent*. McKinsey & Company, Inc. pg. 35.
8. *Corporate Training News*, Winter 2004.
9. "State of the Industry Report," *Training* magazine, October 2003, p. 26.
10. Sugrue B, Kyung-Hyun, K., 2004 ASTD Annual Review of Trends in Workplace Learning and Performance, ASTD, 2004, pg. 4.
11. Benson, G. S., Finegold, D., & Albers Mohrman, S., (2004). "You Paid for the Skills, Now Keep Them: Tuition Reimbursement and Voluntary Turnover." *Academy of Management Journal.* pg. 313–331.
12. Meisler, A., (2004). "A Matter of Degrees." *Workforce Management*, May 2004, pg. 32–38.
13. "Learning Organizations Challenged to Prove Business Impact, Yet Few Do, Accenture Study Finds: Report also Identifies Capabilities of High-Performance Learning Organization." *Business Wire.* New York: Nov. 15, 2004, pg. 1.
14. U.S. Money Markets Report, November 30, 2004. Found at: www.globefund.com.

15. Bernasek, Anna. "Long on Cash, Short on Ideas." Business section, *New York Times*, December 5, 2004, pg. 4.
16. Lawler III, Dr. Edward, Mohrman, Susan Albers. *Creating a Strategic Human Resources Organization*. Stanford University Press, 2003.
17. Bryan, Fraser, Oppenheim, Rall, *Race for the World*, Harvard Business School Press.
18. Michaels, E., Handfield-Jones, H. & Axelrod, B. (2001). *The War For Talent*. McKinsey & Company, Inc. pg. 4.
19. Freedman, Anne. (2003) "Dissatisfaction Down the Line." *Human Resources Executive*. October 2, 2003. pg. 316.
20. Benson, G. S., Finegold, D. and Albers Mohrman S., (2004). "You Paid for the Skills, Now Keep Them: Tuition Reimbursement and Voluntary Turnover." *Academy of Management Journal*. pg. 316
21. Benson, G. S., Finegold, D. and Albers Mohrman S., (2004). "You Paid for the Skills, Now Keep Them: Tuition Reimbursement and Voluntary Turnover." *Academy of Management Journal*. pg. 318
22. Meisler, A., (2004). "A Matter of Degrees." *Workforce Management*, May 2004, pg. 32-38.
23. Appelbaum, S. H., Hood, J. 1993. *The Managerial Auditing Journal* 8: Issue 2, pg. 17.
24. *Encyclopedia Britannica Online* (2004), found at: http://www.britannica.com.
25. *Encarta®World English Dictionary*, North American Edition 2004.
26. Michaels, E., Handfield-Jones, H. & Axelrod, B. (2001). "*The War For Talent.*" McKinsey & Company, Inc. pg. 46.
27. Sherman, Stratford and Alyssa Freas. "The Wild West of Executive Coaching." *Harvard Business Review*, November 2004, pg. 84.
28. Michaels, E., Handfield-Jones, H. & Axelrod, B. (2001). "*The War For Talent.*" McKinsey & Company, Inc. pg. 98.
29. Aslanian, C. (2001). *Adult Students Today*. The College Board, New York, pg. 16.
30. Aslanian, C. (2001). *Adult Students Today*. The College Board, New York, pg. 19.
31. Merrill Lynch, *The Book of Knowledge*, April 9, 1999, pg. 16.

32. Sugrue. B, Kyung-Hyun, K. 2004. "ASTD Annual Review of Trends in Workplace Learning and Performance." ASTD, 2004, pg. 5.
33. Merrill Lynch, *The Book of Knowledge*, April 9, 1999, p. 18.
34. *Encarta®World English Dictionary*, North American Edition 2004.
35. *Merriam-Webster Online Dictionary* (2004) found at: http://www.mw. com.
36. *Cambridge Dictionaries Online* (2004) found at: http://dictionary.cambridge.org.
37. *Merriam-Webster Online Dictionary* (2004) found at: http://www.mw. com.
38. Bartel, A. "Measuring the Employer's Return on Investment in Training: Evidence from the Literature." *Journal of Human Resources* 28: 43–364.
39. *U.S. Census Bureau*, Educational Attainment in the United States: 2003.
40. Benson, G. S., Finegold, D. and Albers Mohrman S., (2004). "You Paid for the Skills, Now Keep Them: Tuition Reimbursement and Voluntary Turnover." *Academy of Management Journal*. p. 319.
41. Benson, G. S., Finegold, D. and Albers Mohrman S., (2004). "You Paid for the Skills, Now Keep Them: Tuition Reimbursement and Voluntary Turnover." *Academy of Management Journal*. p. 315.
42. Benson, G. S., Finegold, D. and Albers Mohrman S., (2004). "You Paid for the Skills, Now Keep Them: Tuition Reimbursement and Voluntary Turnover." *Academy of Management Journal*. p. 315.
43. Meisler, A., (2004). A Matter of Degrees. *Workforce Management*, May 2004, pg. 32–38.
44. Benson, G. S., Finegold, D. and Albers Mohrman S., (2004). You Paid for the Skills, Now Keep Them: Tuition Reimbursement and Voluntary Turnover. *Academy of Management Journal*. p. 328.
45. Aslanian, C. (2001). *Adult Students Today*. The College Board, New York, pg. 16.
46. The session "The Myth of Training ROI" held at the Training 2004 Conference Expo, March 1–3, 2004.

47. Huyett, William J. and Viguerie, Patrick S. "Extreme Competition." *McKinsey Quarterly,* January 24, 2005, pg. 1.
48. Eichinger, R. W. & Lombardo, M. L., (2004) "The ROI on People—The 7 vectors of research." *Lominger,* pg. 5.
49. Michaels, E., Handfield-Jones, H. & Axelrod, B. (2001). *The War For Talent.* McKinsey & Company, Inc. pg. 35.
50. Benson, G. S., Finegold, D. and Albers Mohrman S., (2004). "You Paid for the Skills, Now Keep Them: Tuition Reimbursement and Voluntary Turnover." *Academy of Management Journal.* p. 320.
51. "The High-Performance Workforce Study." *Accenture,* 2002-2003.
52. Huyett, William and Viguerie, S. Patrick, *Extreme Competition,* McKinsey Quarterly, 2005, Number 1, p. 8.
53. Hechinger, John. "U.S. Gets Tough on Failure to Repay Student Loans." *Wall Street Journal,* January 6, 2005, pg. A5.
54. Bukowitz, W. R., Williams, R. L., Mactas, E. S. (2004) Human Capital Measurement. *Research Technology Management.* Washington: May/Jun 2004.47: Iss. 3; pg. 43.
55. Jamrog, J. J., Overholt, M. H., "Building a Strategic HR Function: Continuing the Evolution." *HR. Human Resource Planning.* New York: 2004. 27: Iss. 1; pg. 51.
56. Jamrog, J. J., Overholt, M. H., "Building a Strategic HR Function: Continuing the Evolution. *HR. Human Resource Planning.*" New York: 2004. 27: Iss. 1; pg. 51.
57. Couto, Vinay, Heinz, Imagard, and Moran, Mark J. "Not Your Father's CFO." *Resilience report,* Strategy + Business, Booz, Allen, Hamilton, http://www.strategy-business.com/resilience/rr00016?pg=all, February 2005.
58. (www.cforesearch.com) & www.mercerHR.com/CFO study.
59. Grensing-Pophal, L., (2003). "Human Capital. *Credit Union Management.*" Dec 2003.26: Iss. 12; pg. 54.
60. Michaels, E., Handfield-Jones, H. & Axelrod, B. (2001). *The War For Talent.* McKinsey & Company, Inc. pg. 30.
61. Michaels, E., Handfield-Jones, H. & Axelrod, B. (2001). *The War For Talent.* McKinsey & Company, Inc. pg. 9.
62. *Oxford English Dictionary Online* found at: http://www.dictionary.oed.com/

63. *Cambridge Dictionaries Online* (2004) found at: http://www.dictionary.cambridge.org

64. Dictionary.com found at: www.dictionary.com

65. Sugrue, B., Kyung-Hyun, K. "2004 ASTD Annual Review of Trends in Workplace Learning and Performance." ASTD, 2004, pg. 4.

66. Michaels, E., Handfield-Jones, H. & Axelrod, B. (2001). *The War For Talent*. McKinsey & Company, Inc. pg. 72.

67. Michaels, E., Handfield-Jones, H. & Axelrod, B. (2001). *The War For Talent*. McKinsey & Company, Inc. pg. 75.

68. *Oxford English Dictionary Online* found at: http://www.dictionary.oed.com.

69. *U.S. Census Bureau*, Educational Attainment in the United States: 2003.

70. Benson, G. S., Finegold, D. and Albers Mohrman S., (2004). "You Paid for the Skills, Now Keep Them: Tuition Reimbursement and Voluntary Turnover." *Academy of Management Journal*. p. 323.

71. Benson, G. S., Finegold, D. and Albers Mohrman S., (2004). "You Paid for the Skills, Now Keep Them: Tuition Reimbursement and Voluntary Turnover." *Academy of Management Journal*. p. 324.

72. Hamm, Steve, "LINUX, Inc." *Business Week*. New York: Jan 31, 2005. Iss. 3918; pg. 60.

Index